Beating Anxiety

A Guide to Managing and Overcoming
Anxiety Disorders

TIM WATKINS
For
LIFE SURFING

© Tim Watkins 2013

ISBN-13: 978-1492700302
ISBN-10: 1492700304

CONTENTS

Life Surfing

What is anxiety?

When we speak about "anxiety" or "anxiety disorders", we are often talking about three distinct but interrelated processes:

1. Worry – this is a cognitive process in which your mind thinks about things of concern. Worry can be good when you think your way through a problem to a solution. However, worry can also be bad if it involves "rumination – going over and over the same concern without arriving at an outcome

2. Anxiety – this is the emotion (feeling) that often accompanies worry. It is the feeling that something unpleasant or distasteful is about to happen, and it often triggers avoidance behaviour

3. Stress – is the physical (biological) response to a threat. Our bodies have evolved a "fight or flight" response designed to enhance our physical abilities, narrow our senses and block feelings of pain so that we can either escape or overcome predators.

It is in this sense that "anxiety" is used throughout this guide.

Anxiety, then, involves ordinary human responses to stressful situations and to the *anticipation* of potentially stressful situations.

Every one of us will have experienced anxiety at some time of another. Exams, driving tests, job interviews and first dates are examples of the kind of things that can cause us to have a sleepless night, and to feel anxious and apprehensive beforehand.

Common symptoms of anxiety include:

- Restlessness and agitation
- Racing thoughts
- Increased heart and breathing rate
- Feeling "on edge"
- Muscle tension, aches and pains
- Impaired concentration and memory
- Disrupted sleep
- Stomach "butterflies"
- Urinary frequency

In most ordinary situations, these symptoms are relatively mild and short-lived. Usually, stressful events turn out to be easier than expected. And even if they do go badly, once the event had passed, the anxiety fades with it.

Anxiety disorders are different. In an anxiety disorder the symptoms are much more severe and enduring. They take on a life of their own beyond any stressful event or situation. And, crucially, they interfere with your ability to get on with your day-to-day life.

It is common for people with anxiety disorders to withdraw from social activities as a means of avoiding situations and events that they believe are the cause of anxiety. However, such withdrawal tends to feed on itself—the more you withdraw, the more anxious you become when you have to venture out. This can result in agoraphobia (a fear of public places) and social phobia (a fear of interacting with people) both of which can become severely disabling.

People with anxiety problems also often use "quick fixes" to help them overcome their symptoms. Common quick fixes include substances like:

- o Alcohol
- o Caffeine
- o Chocolate
- o Nicotine
- o Sugar

And behaviours such as:

- o Comfort eating
- o Over-exercising
- o Casual sex / using pornography
- o Excessive shopping
- o Self-harm

These quick fix substances and behaviours all help to relieve the symptoms of anxiety in the short-term, but they come at a high price in terms of increased anxiety problems and poorer health and wellbeing in the longer term.   In many ways, they amount to avoiding rather than confronting, managing and overcoming anxiety.

People affected by anxiety move along a continuum between good and bad mental health. Your place on the continuum will vary from time to time, and will depend upon the severity of your symptoms and the extent to which they prevent you from getting on with, and enjoying, your life.

You may or may not have a formal diagnosis of an anxiety disorder, but if you do, this will cut across the continuum:

Someone can have a diagnosis but, having begun to recover, may be moving toward good mental health. Another person may not have been formally diagnosed, but may still have very poor mental health. And, of course, we all move around the continuum at different times.

Types of anxiety disorder

Phobias

Phobias are the most common type of anxiety, but very
few people with phobias experience symptoms so
severe and enduring that they would qualify for a
clinical diagnosis.

Common phobias include:

- Agoraphobia—fear of public places
- Sociophobia—fear of interacting with other
  people
- Aviophobia—fear of flying
- Animal phobias:
  - Arachnophobia—fear of spiders
  - Chiroptophobia—fear of bats
  - Murophobia—fear of mice
  - Ophidiophobia—fear of snakes
  - Ornithophobia—fear of birds

In fact, think of just about anything and somewhere
someone will have a phobia about it.

It is important to remember that where a phobia is so
severe that it warrants a diagnosis of an anxiety
disorder, then the fear is out of all proportion to any
potential risk involved.   In fact, if you have a phobic
disorder, your anxiety symptoms will be fuelled more
by the fear of how your phobia makes you feel than by
fear of the object of your phobia. Just as the ordinary

feelings of anxiety around an exam or a job interview are worse than the event itself, so, for example, the fear of what arachnophobia feels like is worse than the actual experience of coming face to face with a spider.

Generalised Anxiety Disorder

If you have a generalised anxiety disorder you will experience profound symptoms of anxiety all or most days over a six month period.

The symptoms can be so severe that you may feel that you are "losing control" or that you are "going mad".

This type of anxiety is not linked to any particular situation, but becomes a disabling part of everyday life.

Generalised anxiety usually leads to avoidance behaviour as you try to keep clear of situations and events that you believe will cause you to become anxious. However, this tends to be self-defeating, as the more you try to avoid anxiety, the stronger it becomes.

Using quick fixes (see above) can also make anxiety worse as well as making you generally ill in the long-term.

Panic

Panic is a common symptom of anxiety disorders. A panic attack occurs when the physical and psychological symptoms of anxiety run out of control.

The symptoms of panic are those involved in your body's fight or flight response that has evolved to help you avoid the consequences of extreme danger.

When faced with potential danger, your body responds by shutting down those systems (digestion, broad senses, etc) that are not need to fight or flee, and by boosting those systems (circulation, energy release, pain relief, etc) that you need if you are to survive.

This is experienced as:

- o Rapid heart rate
- o Faster and shallower (upper lung) breathing
- o Narrowing (focused) senses
- o Tightening and warming muscles
- o Crouching (like a boxer or a sprinter preparing to start out of the blocks)
- o Reddening (red and white blotches) of the skin
- o Butterflies in the stomach
- o Desire to urinate
- o Feeling of diarrhoea (during or immediately after extreme danger—such as military combat—people sometimes do evacuate themselves).

The fight or flight response gives you an extra boost to get you out of danger. However, your body can only run it for a short time. If you haven't outrun or fought off the danger in 10 to 15 minutes, you will become exhausted.

Unfortunately, while we have all evolved to (helpfully) respond to external threats, we have also evolved in such a way that we can trigger our fight or flight response just by thinking or worrying about a threat. Moreover, in the modern world, the things that threaten us tend not to be things that can be overcome by fighting or fleeing.

Panic attacks usually occur when your fight or flight response is activated either as an inappropriate response to an external stressor (e.g., being stuck in a supermarket queue), an imagined stressor, or your internal worrying.

Once activated, it is common to respond with even more worry because of feelings such as losing control, becoming ill, going mad, or even that you are going to die—especially if you experience pain in your chest.

This additional worrying about what might be happening causes your fight or flight response to go into overdrive, leading to more worry, leading to more panic. And so it goes on…

Eventually, the response will die down as your body begins to tire. However, in extreme cases, you may experience a series of panic attacks lasting for an hour or more.

If you experience regular episodes involving series of panic attacks lasting for prolonged periods, you may be diagnosed with a Panic Disorder. This is also likely if your experience of panic has impacted upon your life to the point that you are struggling to work or enjoy your life because of your fear of having panic attacks.

Stress Disorders

People who are exposed to traumatic or life-threatening events and situations such as road traffic accidents, fires, disasters and war, can develop profound anxiety in response.

In addition to the common symptoms of anxiety, these disorders often involve reliving the events—sometimes as "flashbacks" in which the event is experienced again. They may also involve feelings of "survivor guilt" in which you feel guilty that you survived or the belief that you could have done more to save others.

In most cases, the initial response to traumatic events is known as "psychic numbing" in which your emotions are closed down in order to help you survive the shock of the trauma.

Symptoms of anxiety in response to trauma are an entirely natural part of the way humans respond to extreme events. Processes such as reliving events, and even having nightmares, are part of the way we incorporate and overcome the event.

Symptoms of anxiety usually develop in the days and weeks after the trauma. Where these symptoms are particularly severe and enduring, you may need

additional medical support, and may be diagnosed with
Acute Traumatic Stress Disorder (ATSD).

Often there will not be an immediate response to the
trauma, and you may be able to get on with your life.
However, sometimes the response can be delayed until
months or even years after the trauma. Where the
symptoms are severe and enduring, this is known as
Post Traumatic Stress Disorder (PTSD).

People with PTSD can face problems where they, and
their doctors, fail to connect the symptoms to the
original trauma. This may lead to their not receiving
specialist support.

Obsessive Compulsive Disorder (OCD)

OCD is a relatively rare anxiety-related disorder that
affects around 1.5 percent of people. It is characterised
by obsessional thoughts, images or impulses
accompanied by compulsive behaviour.

At one time or another, almost everyone will have had a
glimpse of this disorder. In a particularly stressful
situation, you may have engaged in an entirely
unconnected or irrational behaviour in the hope (or
belief?) that this will help things turn out okay. You
may, for example, have crossed your fingers while
making a wish. You may have avoided stepping on the
cracks in the pavement to ward off bad luck. You
might have avoided the number thirteen.

With OCD, the experience is much more severe. The obsessional thoughts, images and impulses are often much more negative and unpleasant. The feeling of anxiety that results from these will be overwhelming, and can only be warded off through the irrational compelled behaviour.

For someone with OCD, the experience is both mentally and physically draining, and socially disabling. At its worst, OCD can result in job loss and relationship breakdown.

As with all anxiety disorders OCD feeds on itself. That is, the more you give in to the anxiety, the stronger the anxiety becomes. This is particularly true during times in your life when you are under stress.

Mixed anxiety and depression

Although doctors classify depression and anxiety disorders as separate illnesses, for many people the two are part of the same problem. Indeed, the experience of mixed anxiety and depression is by far the most common of all mental illnesses for those affected.

Depression is a common condition affecting perhaps 1 in 5 people at some time in their lives. Common symptoms of depression include:

- o   Ongoing sadness and low mood
- o   Feelings of helplessness and hopelessness
- o   Tearfulness

- o Problems with sleep
- o Poor concentration and forgetfulness
- o Loss of enjoyment
- o Loss of sex drive
- o Changes in appetite and weight
- o Feeling anxious or worried
- o Thoughts of self-harm or suicide.

Other less common or less obvious symptoms include:

- o Physical aches and pains
- o Digestive problems
- o Changes to the menstrual cycle.

The main reason for clinicians separating anxiety and depression is to understand how they developed. In many cases, depression develops as an additional (and unhelpful) response to an anxiety disorder. For example, where someone with an anxiety disorder withdraws socially and uses unhealthy quick-fix behaviours in order to (temporarily) overcome their anxiety, this may well result in the development of depression. On the other hand, many people affected by depression also experience some symptoms of anxiety as part of their condition.

Treatment

There are two broad types of treatment for anxiety disorders:

o   Medication
o   Talking therapies.

Both of these are effective, but neither is more effective than the other. As such, the choice of treatment will—in theory—be a matter for discussion between doctor and patient. In practice, however, medication is cheap and available while talking therapies are expensive and, depending on where you live, often involve spending time on a waiting list.

Medication

The National Institute for health and Clinical Excellence (NICE) recommend the use of a Selective Serotonin Reuptake Inhibitor (SSRI) antidepressant such as sertraline as the first treatment for anxiety disorders.

Because of problems with dependency and withdrawal, NICE advise against the use of a benzodiazepine (tranquiliser) for anxiety disorders other than as a short-term response to a particular crisis.

In some cases, a beta-blocker (a drug that regulates your heart rate) may be used in the treatment of a panic disorder.

Although medication will help reduce the symptoms of anxiety, it is unlikely to change the underlying causes of your anxiety. This is something that talking therapies can help with. It is also an area where self-help and self-management are important.

Talking therapies

There are several different types of talking therapies and approaches, each of which can be effective. However, the two main treatments provided by the NHS are counselling and Cognitive Behavioural Therapy (CBT). Both will work with you to help you understand your condition and to modify the thoughts and behaviours that give rise to, contribute to or prolong your anxiety.

Access to talking therapies varies depending on where you live and often on the size of the primary care practice that you are registered with. Larger primary care practices often employ a practice counsellor, while smaller practices have to use a counsellor employed by an external agency, and who may be shared between several practices.

In most parts of England, CBT is provided as part of the Improving Access to Psychological Therapies (IAPT) programme. In Wales, CBT provision varies between health boards, and can involve long waiting times.

Counselling and CBT are available from charities and voluntary groups in some parts of the country. However, waiting times and costs vary. They are readily available privately, and sometimes the costs will be covered by your employer or through private medical insurance.

Life Surfing

Understanding Wellbeing

Most of the focus of treatment within a busy NHS practice is on alleviating symptoms. And while this is important, it is only a staging point on your road to recovery.

Self-help has a different and broader focus. Its concern is with making you well *and keeping you well.* A first step to this is understanding wellbeing.

A helpful model for understanding wellbeing is the image of someone pushing a burden along a slope. There are three factors that affect the ease or difficulty:

- The angle of the slope (is it steep or shallow?) is about the wider environmental, political and economic conditions within which we live.
- The traction of the slope (is it firm or slippery?) represents the various institutions within which we live our lives. These include our families, neighbourhoods, workplaces, schools and colleges, clubs and associations, etc.
- The burden (is it light or heavy?) is about how we are as individuals. It includes our skills and abilities, our beliefs and thoughts, our emotions, our physical bodies, and the way we interact socially.

Someone who has maximum positive wellbeing will be fully engaged socially (at work, at home, in their local community and at play); physically healthy; emotionally balanced, rational and considered; and utilising their core skills and abilities. Their lives will be lived in supportive, nurturing families, neighbourhoods, schools, colleges, workplaces and social associations. These will function within a benign environment, in a free society that delivers economic prosperity and social cohesion.

Of course, few people ever enjoy such a blessed life. Most of humanity is excluded from the benign political and economic conditions enjoyed in Western Europe and the USA in the decades after 1945. Even in these societies, there is no guarantee that social institutions will be nurturing and empowering. Too many people in the UK live in broken families, attend failing schools and live in neighbourhoods where crime and antisocial behaviour are high. Too many employers create and maintain bullying, pressurising, target-driven management cultures that make work insecure and unhealthy for employees.

Nor should we ignore inequalities in health. People born in the UK's poorest communities are shorter, more prone to chronic illness and disability, and likely to die 10 years earlier than those born in the wealthiest areas.

Someone with anxiety is likely to have to struggle with personal factors. Their anxiety will result in:

- Social withdrawal (possibly resulting in unemployment)
- Deteriorating physical health, including:
    - Disrupted sleep
    - Digestive problems
    - Pain
    - Poor diet
    - Lack of exercise
- Poor, often negative, emotional and mental health
- Frustrated core skills and abilities.

Since most anxiety is reactive, these problems are often the result of, or fear of, wider social problems such as:

- Difficulties at work
- Relationship problems
- Being a victim of crime or antisocial behaviour
- Being a carer for a friend or relative.

Anxiety may also be the result of wider economic factors such as:

- Debt
- Redundancy
- Unemployment
- Poverty
- Homelessness

Nor are these factors only the cause of anxiety. In many cases, they also result from anxiety itself. So, for example, someone may develop and anxiety problem after getting into debt. This causes them to withdraw socially, and begins to affect their whole outlook on life. They may develop agoraphobia. This may result in their relationships breaking down, and may cause them to lose their home. The combination of this will make their anxiety worse, making it even harder for them to rebuild their lives.

Recovery from anxiety means taking steps across all of these areas of your life. This means both cutting back on things that make your anxiety worse, and engaging with things that improve your wellbeing. Seen in this way, decisions about both treatment and self-help can be taken in terms of whether they improve or worsen your wellbeing.

This can cause difficulties because there is not a one-size-fits-all approach to treatment and self-help. Antidepressant drugs and talking therapies are effective for most people, but not everyone. And some people find that they add to their problems. Similarly, some people find self-help approaches such as improving diet and engaging in physical activity helps them overcome anxiety and improve their wellbeing. Others find that these things do not help. Some find that they make things work.

Only you can discover what will work for you. This means being prepared to cut back on those things that make your anxiety worse, and trying those things that might help you recover.

Self-help

The aim of most medical treatment is to alleviate of
your symptoms rather than to cure you.
Benzodiazepines (tranquilisers) for example, are used to
give you temporary relief from overwhelming feelings
of distress. Antidepressants are intended to bring about
a longer-term lowering of symptoms, but do nothing to
protect you against relapse when you are faced with
stressful events in future.

One of the reasons behind the growing demand for
talking therapies such as CBT is that they can provide
you with skills that will help you combat the negative,
unrealistic and unhelpful thoughts and beliefs
associated with anxiety disorders. CBT also crosses
into the realm of self-help, as many of the behavioural
elements that a therapist will encourage you to try (e.g.,
relaxation, sleep hygiene, exercise, socialising, etc) are
things that you can easily engage in as part of a self-help
programme.

Self-help is about much more than just the alleviation
of symptoms. It is concerned with your recovery and
with your long term "resilience" (your ability to cope
with life's ups and downs in future without spiralling
down into another episode of anxiety).

Because each of us is different, there is no magic bullet
or miracle cure that you can simply borrow to help
yourself to sustained recovery. Rather, you need to

understand how *your* anxiety operates—what are the things that trigger it? How do you respond to it? Do these responses help or hinder your recovery in the long-term? What else might you do instead?

For example, it is common for people whose anxiety is compounded by low self-esteem resulting from their being over-weight to get into a habit of eating when they become anxious. Their "comfort eating" makes them feel better in the short-term, but leaves them with even greater weight and even lower self-esteem than before. Similar responses apply to people who drink, smoke, take drugs, over-spend or withdraw. In each case, the unconscious habitual response makes them feel good for a brief moment, but adds to their problems in the longer term.

But making changes can seem daunting. There are so many things that might help that it is difficult to know where to start. It is helpful to revisit the model of the components of mental health—someone pushing a burden along a slope.

Self-help involves cutting back on the things that either increase the burden or that make the slope harder to navigate. It also means doing new things that help to shrink the burden and that make the slope easier to travel along.

Because the slope is about things that are beyond individual control, and especially if your anxiety prevents you getting things done, you will have to seek help to deal with them. For example, someone whose problems are triggered or compounded by debt might need the help of an advice agency like Citizens Advice Bureau or an independent law centre (if they are facing legal action). Someone going through relationship problems might benefit from the support offered by Relate. Someone whose problems are made worse by unemployment might benefit from the support of Job Centre Plus or a job broker agency.

However, there are many things relating to your "burden" that you can do for yourself. Above, we set out the components of the burden:

- Social engagement
- Physical health
- Emotional health
- Thoughts & beliefs
- Core skills and abilities.

Notice that the middle three of these relate to the components of anxiety – *stress* is related to physical health, *anxiety* is related to emotional health, and *worry* is related to the health of your thoughts and beliefs. All three are greatly influenced by how you (with your core skills and abilities) relate to and interact with your social surroundings (your work, rest and play).

Most of us do things in each of these areas of our being that stand in the way of wellbeing. This is particularly true for people affected by common mental health problems like anxiety, as there is a great temptation to use quick-fixes that make you feel better in the short-term but make things worse in the long-term. For example:

- o You may make excuses not to go out socially because you are worried about how you will feel
- o You may over-use alcohol because it gives you a temporary sense of calm and relaxation, and because it seems to help you sleep
- o You may experience feelings of guilt, helplessness or hopelessness, and spend time blaming yourself for the way you feel
- o You may think that things will never improve, and act as if this thought were true
- o You may avoid doing things that you have always felt drawn to, or refuse to develop your natural abilities.

These are all examples of "self-sabotage" – they are the type of things that we do that prevent us from improving our mental health and wellbeing. You may be able to think of examples of things that you do that stand in the way of recovery.

There are also many things that people do in each of the areas of their being that can help them overcome common mental health problems and develop sustainable recovery.

Social engagement

Overcoming withdrawal is the most obvious form of self-help. Of course, this is easier said than done, especially if your anxiety involves agoraphobia or social phobia—although these should not be used as an excuse not to do anything (giving in to them only serves to empower them).

Re-engaging socially usually involves a process of "gradual exposure". This involves building up a full social life step-by-step. The starting point will depend on how your anxiety affects you, and what you are currently able to do. If you have (or think you may have) agoraphobia or social phobia, you may want to get professional support with gradual exposure.

Here is an example of how gradual exposure works:

> Tim used to get panic attacks if he tried using a busy supermarket. This resulted in his not using supermarkets and getting other people to go shopping for him. This made shopping more expensive and often meant going without things. Today, Tim doesn't have problems shopping in supermarkets. Here is what he did to get to this point:

1. Use a smaller Metro-type supermarket; shop more frequently for fewer items at a time; go at quiet times of day. Keep doing this until the anxiety subsides

2. Get a friend or relative to take him to a larger supermarket; go at a quiet time of day; use the express check out; get just a few items. Keep doing this until the anxiety subsides

3. Do step 2 on his own until the anxiety subsides.

4. Use a larger supermarket at a quiet time of day, but do a bigger shop and use a regular check out. Keep doing this until the anxiety subsides

5. Repeat stage 4 at a busy time of day. Keep doing this until the anxiety subsides.

Any form of social engagement (from going out with friends to returning to work) can be tackled in the same way.

Of course, we are all different. Some people will need more stages, some will need fewer. And the time that this takes might be weeks, months or even years. This doesn't matter—it isn't a competition. The important thing is that you are on the road to recovery and that each step you take is an achievement along the way.

Physical health

People affected by common mental health problems
often find their physical health deteriorates. Sleep
becomes disrupted, diet changes, more quick-fix
substances (alcohol, caffeine, chocolate, nicotine, sugar,
etc) are consumed, posture goes out of alignment, aches
and pains and digestive problems are common. These
all lead to even more anxiety, resulting in a downward
spiral.

The risk is that there are so many things that you could
do to improve your physical health that you end up
doing nothing, or that you take on far too many things
(and set yourself up to fail). It is more sensible to
choose one or two things that you would like to
improve (choose the ones that seem most appealing to
you) and work just on those.

Physical activity

Our bodies are designed to be active. However, many
modern jobs require us to sit at desks or workstations
for large parts of the day. And for many of us,
recreation time is spent sitting in front of the TV, or
sitting in a bar talking to friends. Those without work
often spend time sitting around at home because they
lack transport and cannot afford many of the activities
that most people take for granted. These kinds of
physical inactivity can become habit forming. They are
also reinforced by stress, which can leave you mentally
drained and can sap any desire to be more active.

Physical activity doesn't have to be expensive. Going for a walk or a jog are free. Cycling is reasonably cheap once you have bought or hired a bicycle. Most local authorities offer lower leisure centre entry fees to people on benefits, pensions or low incomes. Just taking a 30 minute stroll around the block three or four times a week is sufficient to maintain and start to improve your health. Many household and gardening tasks such as cleaning and weeding also count as physical activity.

Daylight & Fresh Air

There is a growing body of evidence that shows that sleep patterns and mood are affected by the amount of daylight we are exposed to. This is a particular problem during the winter, when it gets dark early. It is a major problem for people who work or spend their days indoors—natural daylight is more than 10,000 times stronger than the lights we use in our homes and offices.

Being physically active outdoors is a good way of exposing yourself to daylight.

Relaxation

It used to be thought that relaxation was simply the absence of stress. As such, any activity that isn't stressful (such as watching TV, playing computer games or going to the pub) would count as relaxation. However, as a result of MRI scans, we now know that there is a *relaxation response* that is the opposite of the *fight or flight response* that we experience when we are stressed.

This is important because it means that relaxation is not something that happens passively—it is something that you have to do actively. Our run of the mill mundane activities are usually too passive to generate our *relaxation response*.

Learning to activate your relaxation response can be difficult to begin with. It is a particular problem if you experience anxiety because you will spend more time than normal experiencing the opposite *fight or flight response*. However, getting into a habit of relaxing and using the same techniques at the same time and in the same place as often as possible will help you to develop a relaxation habit.

The simplest thing you could do is to sit, try to concentrate of a single thing (a sound or a smell or a colour or the sensation of your breath) while trying to slow, and not engage with your thoughts. If this proves difficult, you could use a guided relaxation CD (such as the Life Surfing *Distress to De-stress* CD) where you focus on a voice that guides you into relaxation.

You may be able to find a relaxation class locally. Alternatively, you could try attending a class in meditation, tai chi or yoga, as these involve relaxation techniques as part of their practice. Or you could try a complementary therapy such as aromatherapy, massage, reflexology or shiatsu—these can all produce a profound relaxation response.

Sleep

As with relaxation, sleep is a habit that we have to practice (our booklet on sleep goes into much greater detail about this). Sleep becomes disrupted by your stress response not switching off at night, and by a psychological process known as "rumination" in which you worry over and over without coming to a conclusion. This leads to problems getting to sleep; early waking; and tiredness during the day. It is helpful if you can learn not worry about the amount of sleep you are getting. Often even when you think you have been awake all night, you will have actually lapsed in and out of sleep and will have had 4-5 hours of sleep without noticing.

Getting into a sleep routine can gradually help you overcome sleep problems. Simple things such as not having caffeine after 6 o'clock, not going to sleep on a full stomach, and not having a computer or TV on in the bedroom can help. It is also helpful to keep the bedroom clean, tidy, fragrant and at a comfortable temperature.

Diet

There are several ways in which anxiety can affect your diet. Most directly, substances such as alcohol, caffeine, chocolate and sugar contain chemicals provide short-term relief of stress. You may find that you unconsciously reach for food and drink that contain these substances when you are anxious.

Psychologically, you may be inclined to comfort eat as a way of feeling. You may "treat yourself" to a big bar of chocolate, a pack of cream cakes or a tub of ice cream—this is okay once in a while, but it will affect your weight and your general sense of wellbeing if it becomes a habit.

Prolonged anxiety will deaden your senses of smell and taste (this becomes particularly pronounced for people who also develop depression). One result of this is that you may begin to choose foods that are heavily flavoured, salty or sweet. In most cases, these foods are unhealthy and will have a negative impact on your wellbeing in the longer-term.

You may also be tempted to opt for foods (simple carbohydrates like sugar and sweets) that give a quick energy burst by increasing your blood sugar levels. However, the energy burst will be short lived, and you will quickly feel tired again. The alternative is to opt for complex carbohydrates (like oats, potatoes, pasta and rice) that increase your energy levels more slowly, but maintain your energy levels for much longer.

There is a range of foods that are thought to improve mood and energy levels (you can find out more in the Life Surfing guide *Food for Mood*). However, perhaps more important is learning to eat a balanced diet that is low in fat and high in fibre, with plenty of fruit and vegetables.

Emotional Wellbeing

Anxiety is not really about external events – it is about the way you respond.

One of the dangers facing you as you become more anxious is that you turn emotions such as guilt, anger, self-blame and hate in upon yourself. This will impact badly on the way you think and behave.

Learning to manage and express your feelings in a healthy way will help you to improve your resilience to stress in the longer-term.

The most important thing you can do is talk about your feelings. This doesn't mean opening up to anyone irrespective of whether they want to hear about your feelings. Rather, it means finding a trusted friend or relative who will give you the time and space to express how you are feeling.

In the absence of someone close enough to you for you to feel comfortable about expressing your feelings, there are several alternatives:

- o Use a helpline such as Community Advice and Listening Line, Saneline or Samaritans. If you are in employment, your employer may operate a telephone counselling service. You may also have access to telephone counselling if you have medical insurance.

o See if you can access face-to-face counselling. There may be a counsellor based at your local doctors' surgery (although there will most probably be a waiting list). Alternatively, there are many charities that offer counselling. If you have sufficient income, you may want to pay for private counselling—but be aware that the costs can mount up.

o Use online social media to interact with people who have similar issues to you.

You might also want to think about engaging in creative activities that may help you express your feelings less directly. Arts, crafts, music and poetry are all ways in which people can express themselves.

Thoughts and Beliefs

The deeper your anxiety, the more likely you are to develop irrational, unrealistic and often negative thoughts and beliefs. Unfortunately, this is an insidious process that prevents you noticing what is happening.

Unpicking thoughts and beliefs can be difficult to do on your own. This is why it can be helpful to seek counselling or a psychological therapy such as Cognitive Behavioural Therapy (CBT), which can help you develop a more realistic appraisal of your thoughts and beliefs. You may be able to access psychological therapies through your employer if they have an Employee Assistance Programme (EAP). If you are on benefits but seeking to return to work, you may be able to access CBT via JobCentre Plus.

If you are unable to access face-to-face therapy, there is a computerised programme called *Fear Fighter* that is available through the NHS. There are also several online CBT programmes that can be accessed free of charge.

Core Skills and Abilities

We all have things that we are inherently good at. Religious people talk about this in terms of "Mission" (eastern religions have a similar idea embodied in the term "Dharma"). This is the idea that you come into the world with particular purposes to fulfil. The closer you get to achieving these, the greater your sense of wellbeing. If you are not religious or spiritual, you can look at this idea in terms of the effects of the genes that you inherit from your parents. These will determine things like whether you have the ear and manual dexterity to become a musician, the eyes to become a visual artist, or the intellect to become a scientist.

Unfortunately, many of these faculties remain undeveloped and frustrated by our need to make our way in the world. The need to put food on the table takes precedence over learning and practice for many of us. This is often compounded by our upbringing, which in turn shapes our self-beliefs. If you come to believe that you will never be an artist or a musician or a writer or a surgeon, etc, then you will never put in the hours of learning and practice needed to turn these latent talents into developed skills.

Some people are fortunate enough to be able to utilise their skills and abilities in their work. However, for many others, this must be done outside work by participating in hobbies or through involvement in community groups.

It can be difficult to identify those of your skills and abilities that are undeveloped or frustrated. However, a starting point is to understand that when someone is fully engaging their skills and abilities, they develop a sense of *flow*—the feeling that everything is happening easily. This is similar to sportspeople who talk about being "*in the zone*". Think about times in your life when you have felt like this, and think about what you were doing. What were the skills and abilities that you were drawing on? It can help to match these to things that you have always wanted to do (including those that you may have told yourself you would never be any good at).

Of course, even if you can identify your core skills and abilities, there may still be much learning and practice to do before you can develop them. You will also have to decide whether it would be best to pursue them as a career, a hobby or a community activity.

If you can develop and work with your core skills and abilities, you will find that life becomes easier, more enjoyable, and that you are much more resilient in the face of stress.

Lining everything up

The key to overcoming anxiety and developing long-term wellbeing is to adopt healthy approaches to all five of these areas of your being. A person with wellbeing will be socially engaged, physically healthy, aware of her or his emotions, mindful and realistic about his or her thoughts and beliefs, and will be engaging her or his core skills and abilities either through employment, hobbies or through community participation.

In reality, few of us live up to such a high standard. For some, the leap can appear so big that we don't even begin to try.

The important thing is to acknowledge where you are, and work from there. A person who smokes, overeats and drinks too much alcohol is not going to run a marathon any time soon. But they can begin to alter their diet, cut down on the alcohol, and (if they put their mind to it) give up smoking. At the same time, they can go for a walk every evening or do a bit more around the house or in the garden.

Taking things in small, achievable steps is the only way that you can get from where you are to where you want to be. Anything more is just "setting yourself up to fail". Try to do too much and you will just add to the anxiety that you are trying to manage. Remember that even an Olympic marathon runner didn't begin by being able to run 26 miles in less than two hours. Like you, they began by taking a single step.

Life Surfing

About Life Surfing

Life Surfing is a not-for-profit Community Interest Company that was established to provide a coaching, mentoring and training approach for people experiencing common life problems that can cause stress, anxiety and depression.

Our mission is to help people learn to cope with life without the need to call on over-stretched NHS services that are better deployed to help people with severe mental illness.

Over the years we have found that there is a huge amount that people can do to develop their personal resources and to foster their own wellbeing. In most cases, the real need is for encouragement, support, knowledge and skills.

This is what Life Surfing offers.

We have developed a range of services – one-to-one coaching, training workshops, mentoring groups and a range of publications - to give you the knowledge, skills and motivation needed to address life's issues and overcome stress-related problems in a healthy way, and to promote your long-term personal wellbeing.

For further information, please visit the Life Surfing website:

www.life-surfing.com
info@life-surfing.com

Or you can contact us on: 0300 321 4514 / 07922 537 646

Life Surfing
Box 124, R&R Consulting Centre
41 St. Isan Road
Heath
Cardiff CF14 4LW

Life Surfing is a community interest company limited by guarantee (07399335) registered in England and Wales